EARTH, SPACE, AND BEYOND

HOW DO SCIENTISTS
EXPLORE SPACE?

Robert Snedden

Raintree

Chicago, Illinois

www.heinemannraintree.com
Visit our website to find out
more information about
Heinemann-Raintree books.

To order:

☎ Phone 888-454-2279
⌨ Visit www.heinemannraintree.com
to browse our catalog and order online.

Edited by Andrew Farrow, Adam Miller and Adrian
Vigliano
Designed by Marcus Bell
Original illustrations ©Capstone Global Library 2011
Illustrated by KJA-artists.com
Picture research by Hannah Taylor
Originated by Capstone Global Library Ltd.
Printed in the United States of America in North
Mankato, Minnesota. 032016   009604RP

18 17 16
10 9 8 7 6 5 4 3

Library of Congress Cataloging-in-Publication Data
Snedden, Robert.
  How do scientists explore space? / Robert Snedden.
    p. cm.—(Earth, space, and beyond)
  Includes bibliographical references and index.
  ISBN 978-1-4109-4158-9 (hc)—ISBN 978-1-4109-4164-0
(pb) 1. Astronomy—Juvenile literature. 2. Astronomy—
Observations—Juvenile literature. 3. Comets—Juvenile
literature. 4. Asteroids—Juvenile literature. 5. Outer
space—Exploration—Juvenile literature. I. Title.
  QB46.S686 2012
  520—dc22   2010040158

Acknowledgments
The author and publishers are grateful to the following
for permission to reproduce copyright material: Corbis
pp. 4 (©Reuters/ HO), 16 (©REUTERS/NASA-Johns
Hopkins University Applied Physics Laboratory/Carnegie
Institution of Washington), 19 (©kyodo/XinHua/Xinhua
Press), 20 (©Reuters), 28 (©Reuters TV), 31 (©NASA),
36 (©NASA/ STScI), 37 (©NASA/ STScI), 38 (©epa);
Corbis SABA p. 9 (©Najlah Feanny); Getty Images p. 5
(amana images); ©Justin Knight p. 33; NASA pp. 8, 12
(JPL), 13 (JPL-Caltech), 14, 18 (JPL), 21 (JPL-Solar System
Visualization Team), 22, 23, 29, 30, 32 (ESA/ G.Bacon),
34, 40 (PIRL/University of Arizona); Science Photo Library
pp. 6, 7 (©European Space Agency/ DLR/ Fu Berlin
[G.Neukum]), 10 left (©Gemini Observatory/NOAO/
AURA/NSF), 10 right (©NASA), 24 (©European Space
Agency), 25 (©European Space Agency), 26 (©NASA),
39 (©Walter Myers); SETI p. 41; Shutterstock p. 15 (©
Christian Darkin).

Cover photograph of astronaut in space reproduced with
permission of NASA.

We would like to thank Professor George W. Fraser for his
invaluable help in the preparation of this book.

Every effort has been made to contact copyright holders
of any material reproduced in this book. Any omissions
will be rectified in subsequent printings if notice is given
to the publisher.

Disclaimer
All the Internet addresses (URLs) given in this book were
valid at the time of going to press. However, due to the
dynamic nature of the Internet, some addresses may
have changed, or sites may have changed or ceased to
exist since publication. While the author and publisher
regret any inconvenience this may cause readers, no
responsibility for any such changes can be accepted by
either the author or the publisher.

EARTH, SPACE, AND BEYOND

HOW DO SCIENTISTS EXPLORE SPACE?

Contents

Some words are shown in bold, **like this**. You can find out what they mean by looking in the glossary. You can also look out for them in the "Word Station" box at the bottom of each page.

Sky Watchers

The earliest space explorers were the first people who looked up at the night sky and wondered about the things they saw. The beginnings of space exploration took place from the ground with no more sophisticated tools than sharp eyes and inquiring minds.

These immense columns of gas and dust are big enough to swallow our entire solar system many times.

Ancient astronomers imagined patterns connecting the stars in the sky. These patterns are called constellations.

Fixed stars

The first sky watchers would have noticed that most of the objects in the night sky always kept the same positions relative to each other. They rose and set in orderly patterns that always stayed the same. People of different countries, such as the Greeks, Chinese, and Indians, named these patterns of stars after gods and heroes. The night sky became a storybook of myths and legends.

Wandering stars

The sky watchers of long ago also saw that there were some objects that didn't follow regular paths. The ancient Greeks called them *planetes* (wanderers) from which we get our word *planet*. The early observers built up precise records of the movements of stars and planets across the night sky. These observations became the basis of the modern science of **astronomy**, the study of everything that lies beyond the Earth's **atmosphere**.

Aristarchus

Aristarchus, who lived over 2,200 years ago, was one of the greatest **astronomers** of ancient Greece. He used his observations to work out the sizes and distances of the Sun and Moon. He had no sophisticated instruments with which to make measurements and the answers he got were wrong, but his methods were correct. He correctly worked out that the Sun was very much bigger than the Earth and believed that the Earth moved around the Sun. It would be almost 1,800 years before that idea was accepted.

Navigation

The patterns of stars are called **constellations**. First labeled in ancient times, modern astronomers still use constellations as a convenient way to divide and describe the night sky.

We can also use the stars to find out where we are on Earth. For example, for centuries people have known that facing Polaris, the North Star, means that they are facing north. Hundreds of years ago sailors had starcharts that told them how far above the horizon a star should be. Measuring the angle of the star above the horizon told them how far north or south they were.

Where are the Martians?

Even looking through a powerful telescope the planet Mars looks no bigger than a golf ball. It is hard to see much surface detail. Astronomers such as the Italian Giovanni Schiaparelli (1835–1910) and the American Percival Lowell (1855–1916) studied Mars through telescopes and saw channels, or *canali* in Italian, stretching out over the planet. Lowell was sure these were man-made canals, evidence that there was intelligent life on Mars. Other astronomers disagreed, but very soon the idea of walking, talking Martians became part of popular culture. Belief in Martians like these was finally put to rest when the space probe Mariner 4 reached Mars in 1965. It sent back pictures of an empty and barren landscape, covered in craters.

The telescope

Space exploration took a great leap forward with the invention of the telescope. As telescopes became more and more powerful, previously unseen wonders of the **Universe** opened up before the astounded eyes of astronomers.

The scientist Galileo Galilei (1564–1642) constructed one of the very first telescopes in 1609. Compared to modern telescopes it was not very powerful. After some experiments, Galileo improved the magnification from 3 times to 20 times, which is similar to the power of telescopes used by birdwatchers today. However, using it Galileo discovered mountains on the Moon and spots on the Sun.

Percival Lowell drew this sketch of Mars. He was convinced that he saw canals crossing the planet's surface.

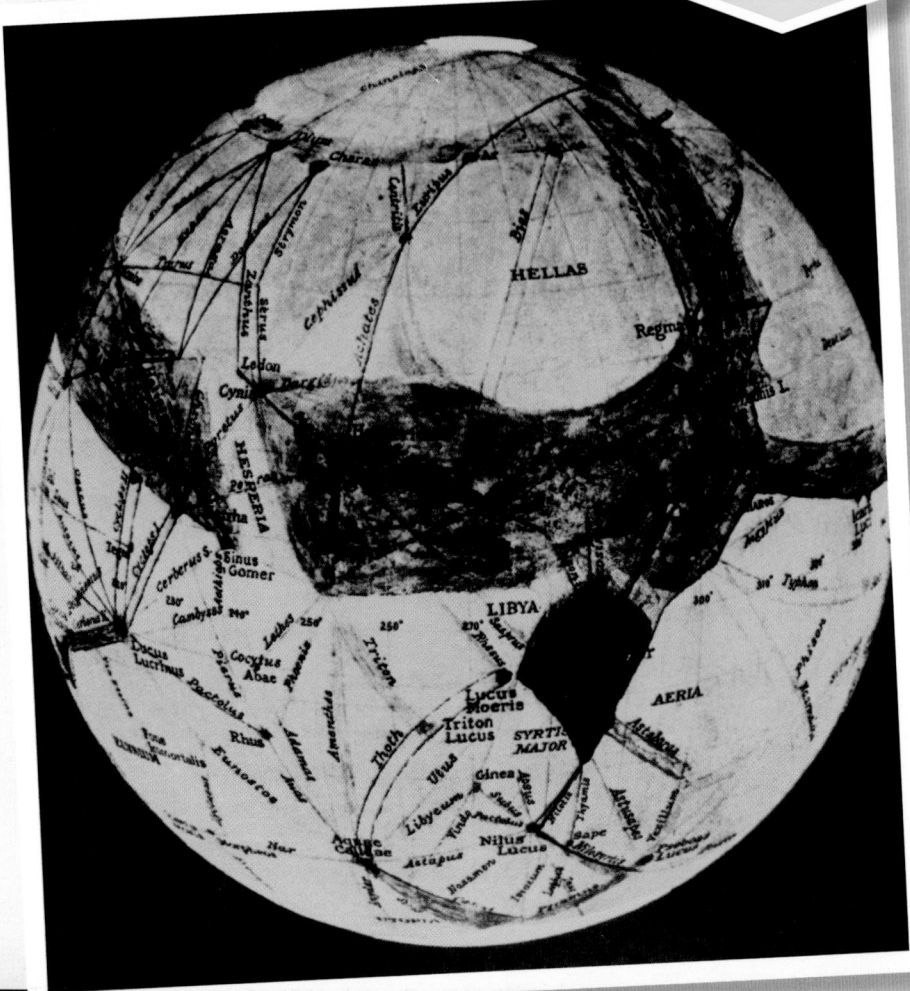

Most amazing of all, Galileo discovered that the planet Jupiter had moons of its own. At that point it was widely believed that everything in the Universe rotated around the Earth. The moons of Jupiter were proof that this was not the case.

Limits to seeing

Over the next three to four hundred years telescopes went on getting bigger and better, and astronomers went on making new discoveries about the Universe. However there is one important thing that limits what can be seen with a telescope — Earth's atmosphere. As light passes through the gases and dust in the atmosphere it gets distorted. This is why major telescopes are built on mountains. Because of pollution, the higher up you are, the clearer the air is.

The Mars Express probe took this photograph of an ancient Martian riverbed. There has not been any water on Mars for billions of years.

Universe everything that exists; all of space and everything it it

Telescopes in space

In 1990, space scientists realized their dream of rising above the problems caused by the atmosphere. This was when the Hubble Space Telescope was put into **orbit** around the Earth.

The Hubble Space Telescope in orbit, as seen by a visiting space shuttle crew.

Hubble Space Telescope

The Hubble Space Telescope was carried into orbit aboard the space shuttle *Discovery* in April 1990. After another shuttle mission fixed the problems with its main mirror, Hubble began to send pictures back to Earth. The results were astounding, showing startling images of the furthest reaches of the Universe.

Dr. Heidi Hammel of the Space Science Institute in Boulder, Colorado, is just one of many scientists who have made good use of Hubble's abilities. She used the telescope to see what happened to Jupiter in July 1994 when it was struck by a **comet**. "We discovered that it made a huge effect on the planet, from big black spots, to vast plumes of ejected material, to waves rippling through the atmosphere."

A number of shuttle missions have returned to Hubble over the years to replace parts that have failed and to keep its equipment up to date. Even so, Hubble's replacement, the James Webb Space Telescope is already being prepared for launch in 2014.

James Webb Space Telescope

More than 1,000 people in 17 countries are currently developing the James Webb Space Telescope. The telescope will have a giant mirror 6.6 meters (21.7 feet) across that will collect the faint light from the most distant objects in space (Hubble's main mirror is less than half that size). Getting a mirror this big into space is a challenge. The Webb team came up with a design using 18 hexagonal (six-sided) segments made of a material that is light, yet strong. The segments will be folded up to fit inside the rocket launcher. Once the telescope reaches orbit the mirror will unfold and observations can begin.

Dr. Heidi Hammel has made excellent use of Hubble to study Jupiter. She will also be involved with the new James Webb Space Telescope.

Looking beyond light

We can see things in space because of the light that reaches our eyes from these distant objects. Stars produce their own light, and planets, moons, and other objects reflect light. When we see the Moon at night it is reflecting light from the Sun towards the Earth.

However, visible light is not the only type of energy given off by objects in space. Light is just a part of the **electromagnetic spectrum**, a range of different types of energy that travel through space in the form of waves.

Radio astronomy

The longest electromagnetic waves are radio waves. Radio astronomers use radio telescopes to look deep into space. They explore giant **black holes** at the heart of **galaxies** and the dusty regions of space that light cannot pass through, where new stars are formed. It is possible to link up the signals from more than one radio telescope so that they act as if they were one huge telescope. This makes them incredibly powerful instruments for exploring the Universe.

Cold stars

The Spitzer Space Telescope (see page 11) discovered some of the coldest stars in the Universe. They are called brown dwarf stars and they are so cold and faint that ordinary light telescopes cannot see them. Some are as cool as 180°C (350°F), which is about the same temperature as a hot oven.

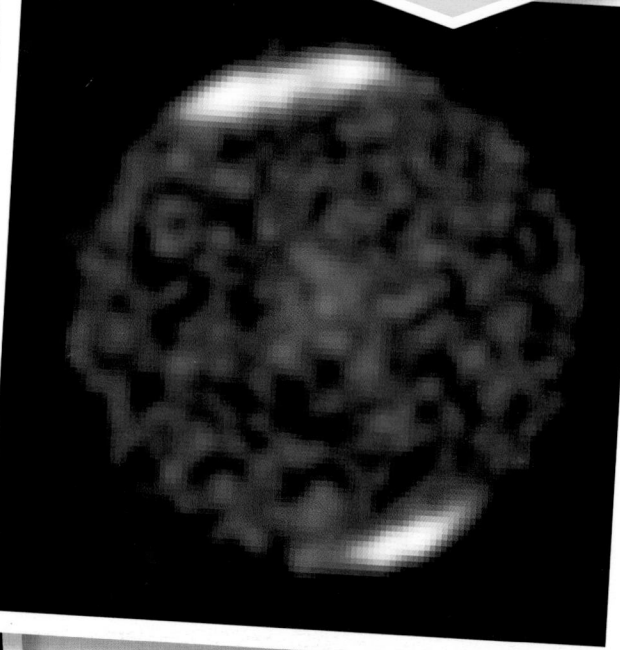

Two views of the planet Jupiter: on the left as it appears in infrared, and on the right as an X-ray image.

Infrared astronomy

We cannot see infrared waves, but we can feel them as heat. The warmth of the Sun comes from infrared radiation. Very little infrared radiation makes it through the atmosphere to reach the surface of the Earth, but scientists are making new discoveries by using infrared telescopes in space, such as the Spitzer Space Telescope.

X-ray astronomy

At the furthest end of the electromagnetic spectrum are the high-energy X-rays and gamma rays. The atmosphere absorbs nearly all of these high-energy waves from space, so X-ray astronomy wasn't possible until the invention of satellites. The X-ray universe turned out to look very different from the visible universe. Because X-rays are high energy it is mainly very hot objects in space, such as exploding stars, that are able to produce them.

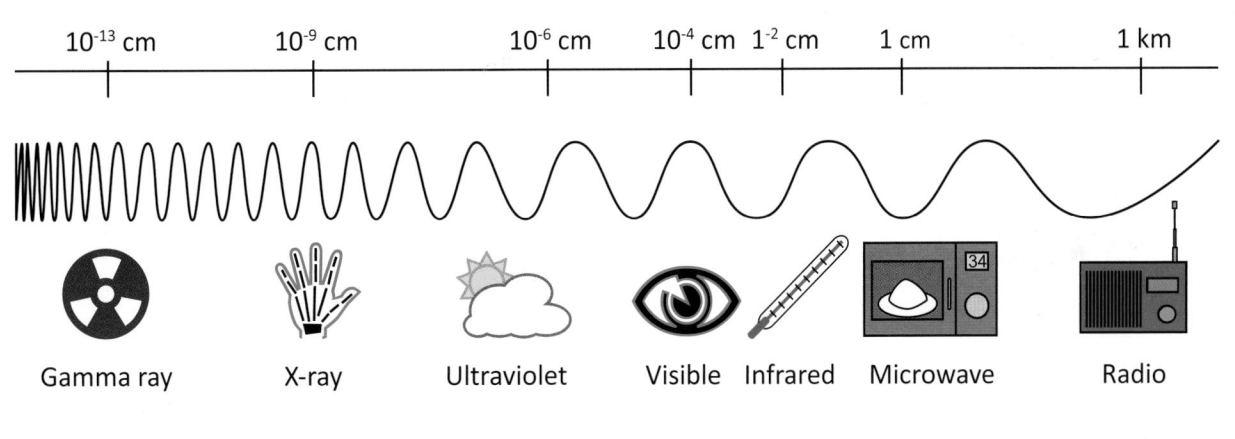

The electromagnetic spectrum is the name for a range of different types of energy that travel through space in the form of waves. Some of these waves, light waves, are visible to us but the others are not. All of these forms of energy are given off by various objects in space. Using special instruments that can detect these waves, astronomers can build up a picture of the Universe that is richer than would be possible with our eyes alone.

WORD STATION
black hole region of space left by a star collapsing; gravity in a black hole is so strong not even light can escape it

11

Project Planet

Planetary scientists investigate planets and their moons. They are interested in the processes that formed these objects and in the forces that continue to shape them today.

Up until the middle of the twentieth century, all of these investigations were carried out using powerful telescopes, both optical and radio. Everything changed when rockets that could send probes out into space became available.

The planet Mars as photographed by Mariner 4. This is one of the first images of another planet to be sent back from space.

This image is an artist's impression of Voyager 1 as it travels through deep space.

Voyager's journey

One of the most successful probes is Voyager 1, which returned images of the giant planets Jupiter and Saturn and their moons in 1979 and 1980. Thirty years later Voyager is the most distant probe from Earth and is still working. As it heads towards **interstellar space** it continues to send back information about the furthest reaches of the solar system. Voyager is so far away that it takes a signal from the spaceship almost sixteen hours to reach Earth. Space scientists expect Voyager to keep operating until at least 2025.

First probes

The first **space probe** from Earth to reach another planet was Mariner 2, which flew within 35,000 kilometers (22,000 miles) of Venus in 1962. Since then a huge number of probes have gathered information on all of the major planets in the **solar system** and their moons.

Space probes changed the way we think about the other planets in space. Once they were little more than lights in the sky. Now they were places, whole new worlds, we had been to and begun to explore. Space probes have given planetary scientists the opportunity to see these distant worlds in a wealth of detail that could never have been possible from Earth.

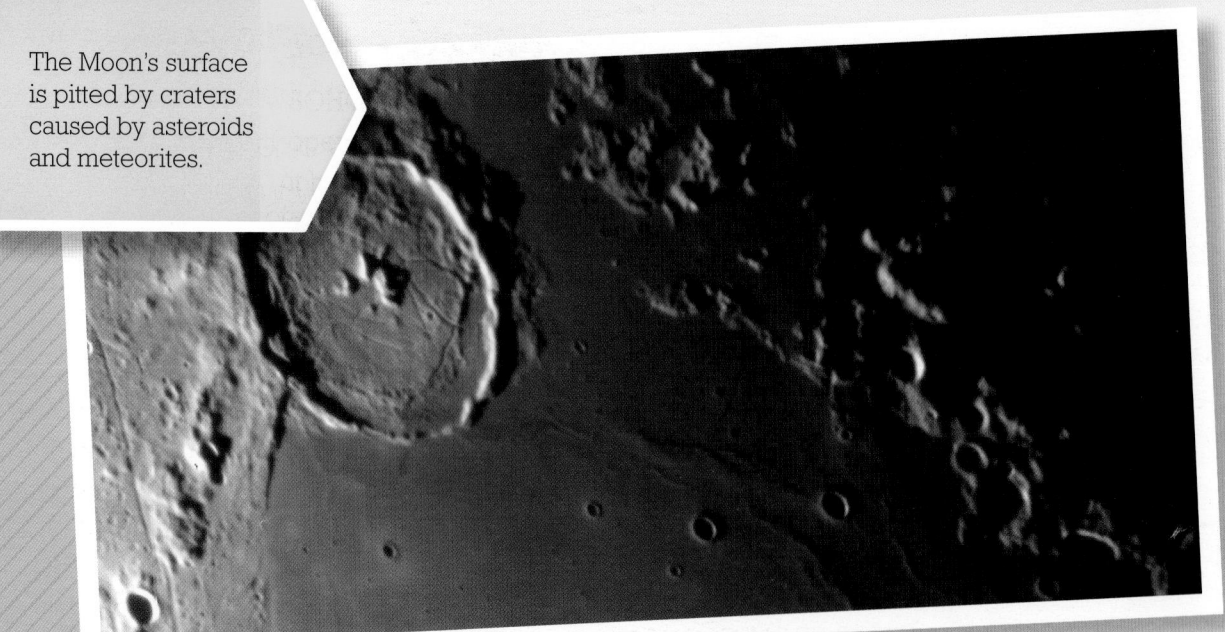

The Moon's surface is pitted by craters caused by asteroids and meteorites.

From the Earth to the Moon

The closest object to us in space is the Moon. It is the brightest object in the night sky and the only one that is close enough for surface details to be seen clearly through a telescope. The Moon has a special position in the history of space exploration. It is the only other place in the Universe that people from Earth have visited.

Project Apollo

Project Apollo was the American space program that first landed people on the Moon between 1969 and 1972. The Apollo missions discovered several things about the Moon that couldn't have been discovered from Earth.

Samples of rock were brought back to Earth. Examining these rocks told scientists that the Moon has always been lifeless. No trace of any life has ever been found in the Moon rocks.

Studying the rocks also showed that the youngest Moon rocks are nearly as old as the oldest Earth rocks. In its earliest history the whole surface of the Moon was an ocean of molten rock. These findings support the idea that the Moon was formed when another object collided with the young Earth, throwing huge amounts of debris into space. This debris gathered together to form the Moon.

Over millions of years, **asteroids** and **meteorites** pounded the Moon. The surface of the Moon is covered in a layer of dust and rubble left by those crashes. Because there is no air or water on the Moon there is nothing to erode the rocks or wash the dust away.

The first space bases on the Moon will be small, with just a few buildings to support scientific study and exploration.

Robots to the Moon

India, China, and Japan have all successfully sent probes to the Moon in recent years. Japan is currently developing plans for a Moon base that will be operated by robots.

The first of the 300-kilogram (661-pound) robots is scheduled to arrive on the Moon by 2015. They will roam around the lunar surface on caterpillar treads. Their equipment will include **solar panels**, from which they will get their power,

high definition cameras, and a variety of scientific instruments. The robots will collect samples to be sent back to Earth by rocket. The next stage of the plan is for the robots to build a solar-powered Moon base near the south pole of the Moon by 2020. At that point astronauts might join the robots. Japan's scientists believe that a Moon base will be an essential jumping-off point from which to explore the solar system.

Messenger to Mercury

Mercury is the closest planet to the Sun. The glare from the Sun makes it very difficult to observe Mercury. So far, only two spacecraft from Earth have visited Mercury, the smallest planet in the solar system. Until space scientists saw the pictures they sent back they had little idea what the surface of Mercury looked like.

Slingshot through space

The first craft to reach Mercury was Mariner 10, launched in 1973. It was also the first spacecraft to make use of something called a **gravity assist**, or slingshot. Scientists have discovered that if a probe passes by a planet at just the right angle, the planet's **gravity** can be used to change its speed and direction. Mariner 10 used Venus to slow down on its way to Mercury, saving rocket fuel.

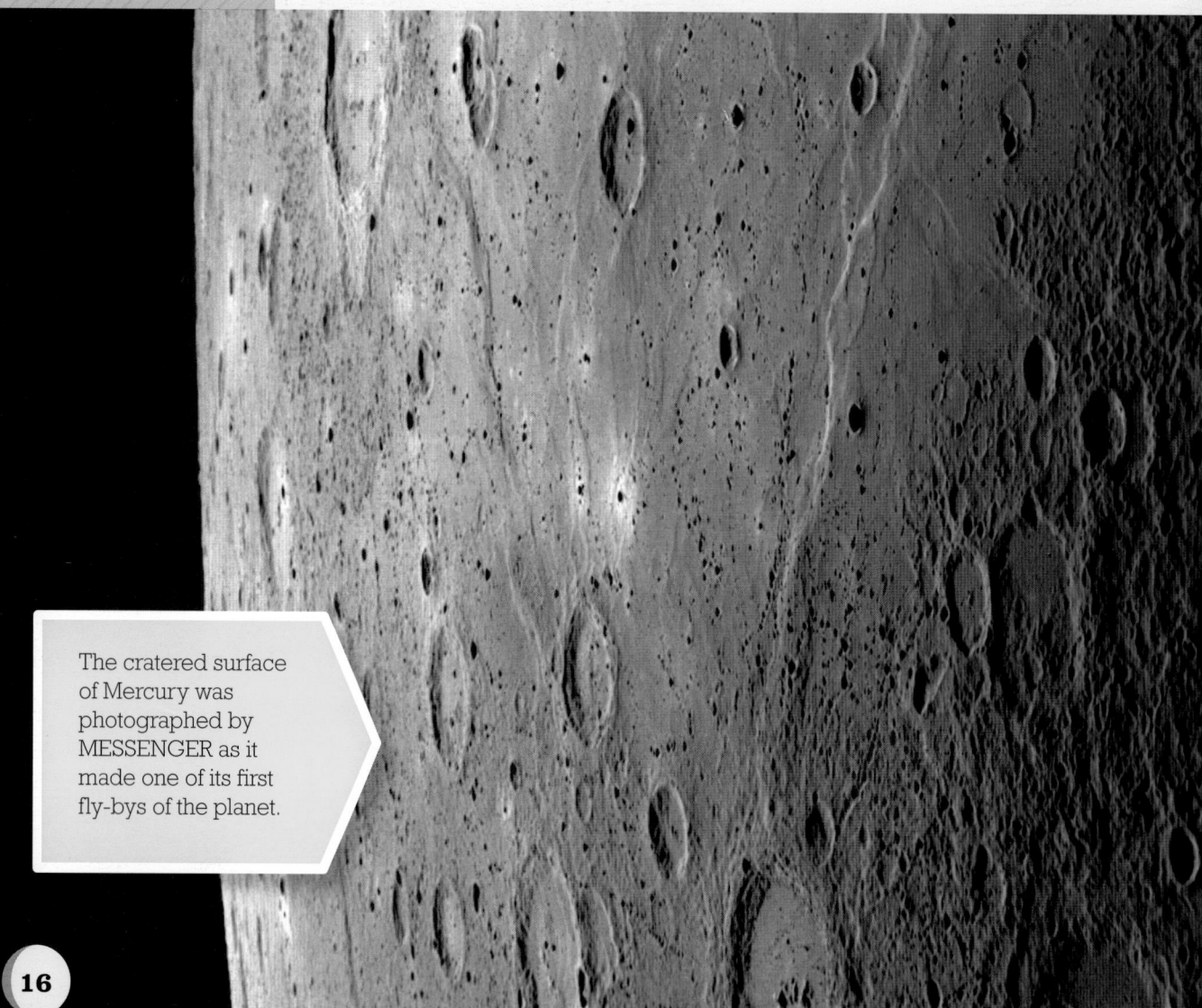

The cratered surface of Mercury was photographed by MESSENGER as it made one of its first fly-bys of the planet.

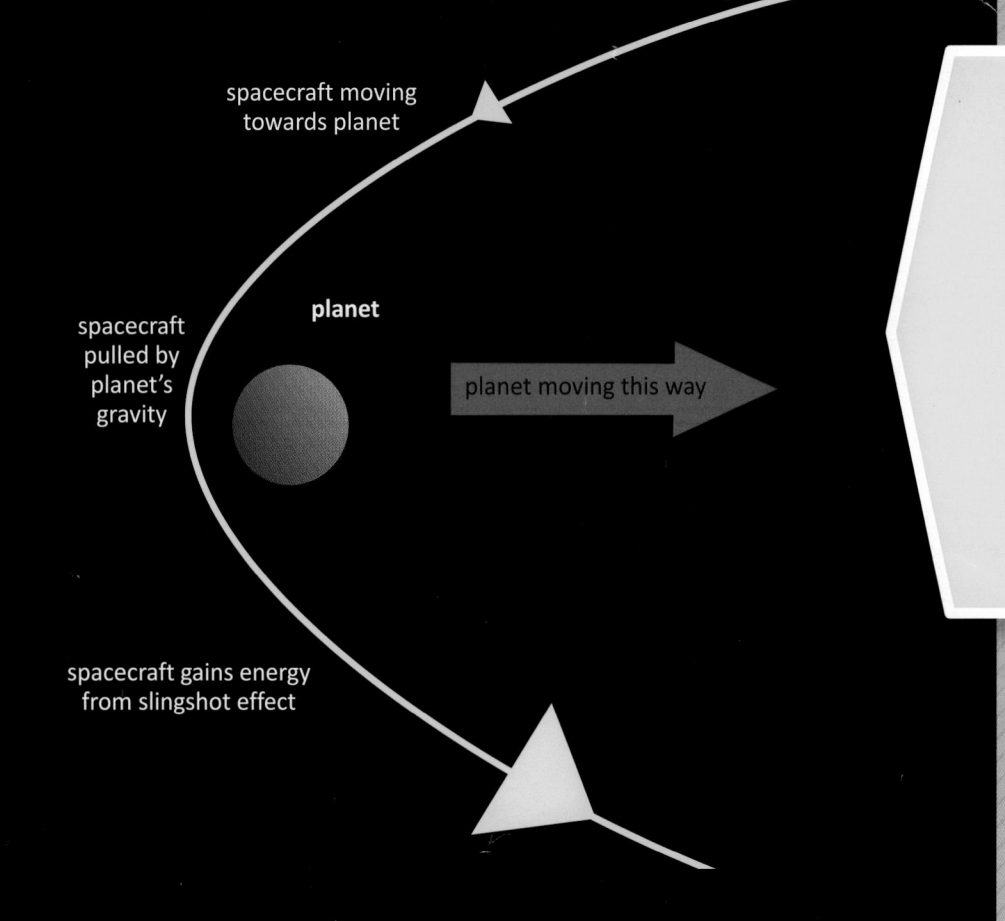

spacecraft moving towards planet

planet

spacecraft pulled by planet's gravity

planet moving this way

spacecraft gains energy from slingshot effect

A spacecraft approaching a planet is pulled towards the planet by the planet's gravity. If the approach is made at the right angle the craft can use the planet's gravity to change course and speed. This slingshot maneuver saves valuable rocket fuel.

MESSENGER

MESSENGER (the MErcury Surface, Space ENvironment, GEochemistry, and Ranging) spacecraft will be the first satellite to be placed in orbit around the planet Mercury. MESSENGER is on a complex looping, energy-saving flight path that sees it flyby the Earth once, Venus twice, and Mercury three times before finally entering orbit around Mercury in March 2011. It takes a long time to reach Mercury by this route. However, it means that the spacecraft doesn't have to carry the large amounts of rocket fuel that would otherwise be needed to slow it down enough to enter orbit.

Louise Prockter is the lead instrument scientist for the Mercury Dual Imaging System (MDIS) carried aboard MESSENGER. The MDIS will help Prockter and the rest of the team investigate the different rock types on Mercury. She was one of the first to see the surface of an asteroid — now she's looking forward to a close-up view of Mercury.

"The pace of the mission can get quite hectic. The spacecraft keeps moving no matter what's going on in your life, and balancing all that can be a challenge."

Louise Prockter

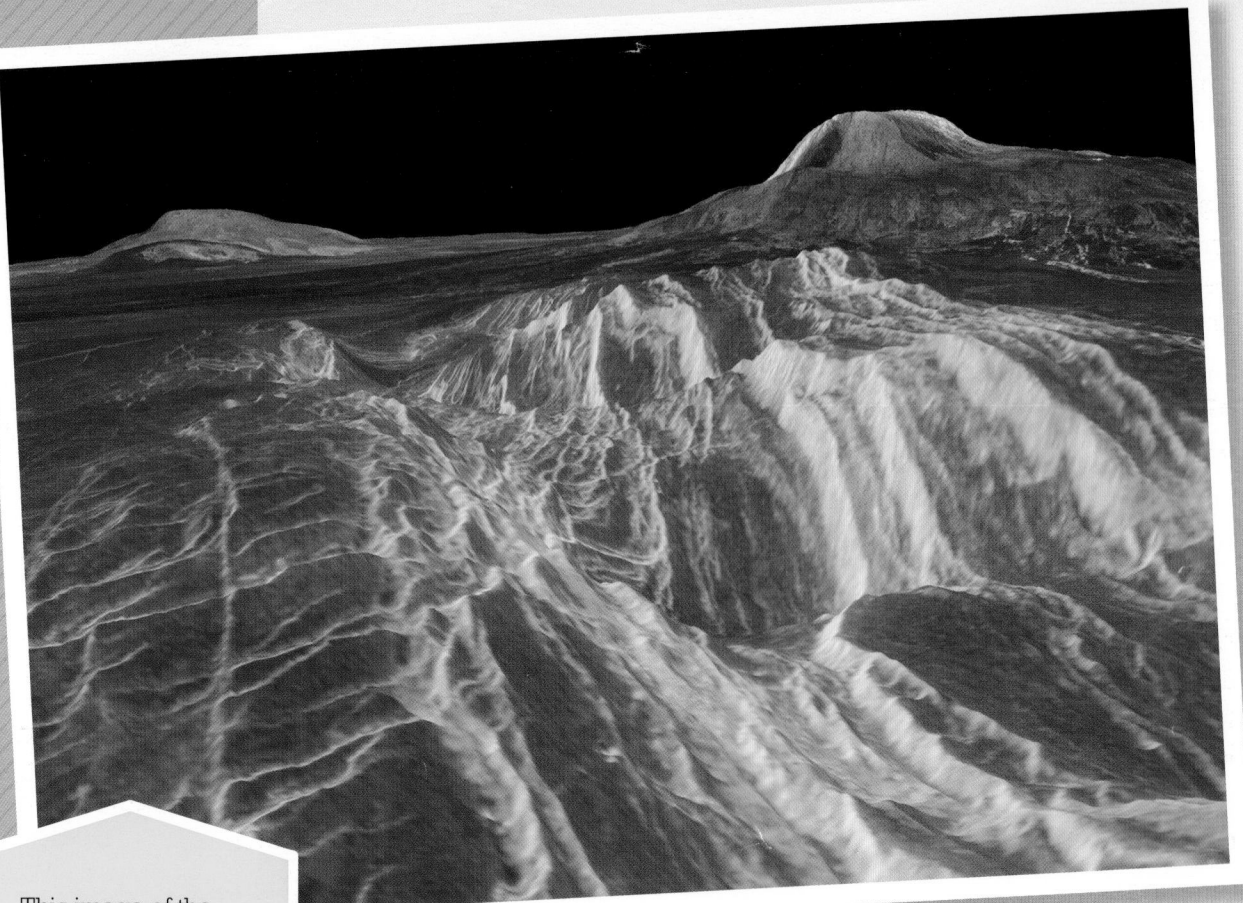

This image of the surface of Venus was created using radar images taken from the Magellan space probe.

Venus weather watch

We are used to seeing satellite reports of the weather here on Earth. Now there is a mission to take a look at the weather on another planet.

Akatsuki

The Japanese space probe Akatsuki (originally called the Venus Climate Orbiter) was launched on May 21, 2010, and was scheduled to enter orbit around Venus in December 2010, but failed to do so. Scientists will try again to enter it into orbit, but they will have to wait six years while Akatsuki travels once around the Sun! If they are successful, Akatsuki will be one of the first weather satellites to orbit another planet.

One of the things Akatsuki will try to explain are the ferocious storm winds that blow across the surface of the planet. These rage around Venus at speeds of over 360 km/h (220 mph). Called super-rotation, the winds travel sixty times faster than the planet itself rotates. At the moment scientists don't know what might be causing this.

On board Akatsuki are infrared cameras that can peer through the thick atmosphere to the surface of the planet. It is hoped that they might reveal the cause of the high-speed winds. Project scientist Takeshi Imamura is open-minded about what may be discovered. "We may be pleasantly surprised by the emergence of a greater mystery than super-rotation," he said.

Satellite partnership

When Akatsuki reaches Venus it will join the European Space Agency's Venus Express, which is already in orbit studying the chemicals in the planet's atmosphere.

"Venus Express and Akatsuki are like sister satellites, and a very good cooperative relationship has been built as we have progressed in our missions," Imamura said. David Grinspoon, one of the Venus Express scientists, agrees. "Venus [is] a really dynamic planet that's very changeable. Having Akatsuki there should help capture more vital clues to understanding Venus's mysteries."

Global warming

Venus is similar in size to the Earth, but conditions there are very different. A thick carbon dioxide atmosphere blankets its barren desert landscape. Venus is hotter than Mercury, even though it is farther from the Sun. Many scientists are concerned that the Earth's temperature is rising. Is Venus a warning for the future?
Carbon dioxide is a **greenhouse gas**. The heat it traps has boosted the surface temperature of Venus to a sweltering 480°C (900°F). By studying conditions on Venus scientists hope to understand how conditions here on Earth might be changed if the amount of carbon dioxide in our atmosphere increases.

A rocket carrying the Akatsuki space probe lifts off from Japan's Tanegashima Space Center.

A day on Mars

A day on Mars

A Martian day is called a **sol** and Mars mission scientists measure the time a probe has been on the surface in sols rather than days. One Martian sol is 35 minutes, 39 seconds longer than one day on Earth.

Red planet rovers

Scientists have sent a number of probes to land on the surfaces of other worlds. Landers have visited the Moon, Venus, Mars, Saturn's moon Titan, and even an asteroid. Two of the most successful of these surface explorers have been the Mars Exploration Rovers, called Spirit and Opportunity.

Martian mission

The Mars rovers arrived on Mars in January 2004. Their main mission is to sample as wide a range of rocks and soils on the surface as possible. Scientists have found evidence that water once flowed on Mars. This water might have made it possible for life to exist on Mars long ago.

This artwork shows one of the Mars Exploration Rovers emerging from its protective capsule after landing on the surface of Mars.

Sunset on Mars. The Sun appears smaller than it does on Earth because Mars is much further from the Sun than Earth is.

Setting a course

When the rovers first arrived they took panoramic (full view) pictures of their surroundings. This helped the scientists to pick out places that looked worth investigating. Deciding on a rover's route across the Martian surface takes careful planning. Once the scientists have decided on their targets the engineering team has to determine whether or not the rover can get there safely.

It takes twenty minutes for a radio signal to travel across space from Earth to Mars, so it is impossible to steer the rover in "real time." At the start of each day a set of instructions is uploaded to the rover. These instructions tell the rover where to go and what experiments to carry out.

Avoiding hazards

The rover is equipped with hazard avoidance software. Every few seconds the rover stops and examines the surface in front of it using a pair of Hazcams (hazard cameras). If there is a possible hazard ahead the on board computer will instruct the rover to change course to avoid it.

Rover update

The Mars rovers have kept going far longer than scientists expected. By summer 2010, Spirit had powered down and contact had been lost. Scientists hope to regain contact when its batteries recharge using its solar panels. Opportunity is still going strong and continues to send back information.

Juno to Jupiter

The planets are not unchanging objects in space. Early in 2010 one of the two main cloud belts that circle the giant planet Jupiter completely disappeared. The Southern Equatorial Belt (SEB) is more than twice as wide as the entire planet Earth. Yet every now and then it vanishes, only to mysteriously reappear in a dramatic outburst of storms that circle Jupiter.

Planetary scientists would love to know why this happens. Planetary scientist Glenn Orton thinks that the cloud belt might not have disappeared. It is possible that is hidden beneath other clouds that have formed above it. Orton has suggested that changing wind patterns on Jupiter have caused high-altitude clouds to form and cover up the cloud belt. But no one can explain why the southern belt should vanish while the northern belt remains.

> "We have a long list of questions."
>
> **Glenn Orton**

These photographs clearly show that Jupiter's Southern Equatorial Belt of clouds has disappeared.

Jupiter

Before
August 4, 2009

After
May 8, 2009

The Juno space probe is shown here being fitted with a heavy shield to protect it from Jupiter's radiation.

Juno

NASA's Juno probe, due for launch in 2011, may provide some of the answers. The journey from Earth to Jupiter will take five years.

Juno's highly sensitive instruments will map Jupiter in several different ways. It will measure its powerful magnetic field and strong gravity. It will look at Jupiter's atmosphere to see how it varies from place to place across the planet. No one knows how deeply the features we see on Jupiter actually go. Juno will probe deep beneath the clouds to find out what is going on inside Jupiter's atmosphere. Perhaps here it will find reasons for the mysterious vanishing cloud belt.

First views

When it arrives, Juno will enter an orbit that will take it over the poles of the biggest planet in the solar system. It will have views of Jupiter that have never been seen before. Amongst Juno's complex scientific instruments there is a color camera. This was included to give people their first view of Jupiter's poles.

Comet Encounters

The Kuiper belt

In 1951, after studying the paths followed by many comets, astronomer Gerard Kuiper suggested that there must be a belt of perhaps hundreds of millions of comets out beyond the orbit of the planet Neptune. In 1992, astronomers detected a **Kuiper belt** object (KBO) for the first time. Today more than 1,300 KBOs have been identified.

Comets are icy remnants left over from the formation of the planets. Some travel on orbits that take them in towards the Sun then back out to the outer solar system. As the comet approaches the Sun, radiation heats it. This causes gas and dust to boil off, forming the comet's distinctive tail.

Rosetta

The European Space Agency's Rosetta probe will be the first to explore a comet at close range over a long period of time. It is currently on its way to meet with Comet 67P/Churyumov-Gerasimenko in 2014. Rosetta will receive gravity assists from both Earth and Mars to speed it on its long journey.

When it arrives, the spaceship will go into orbit around the comet. It will spend the next two years accompanying the comet as it heads towards the Sun. A small lander will also be placed on the surface of the comet. A number of scientific experiments carried on board the orbiter and lander will carry out the most detailed study of a comet ever attempted.

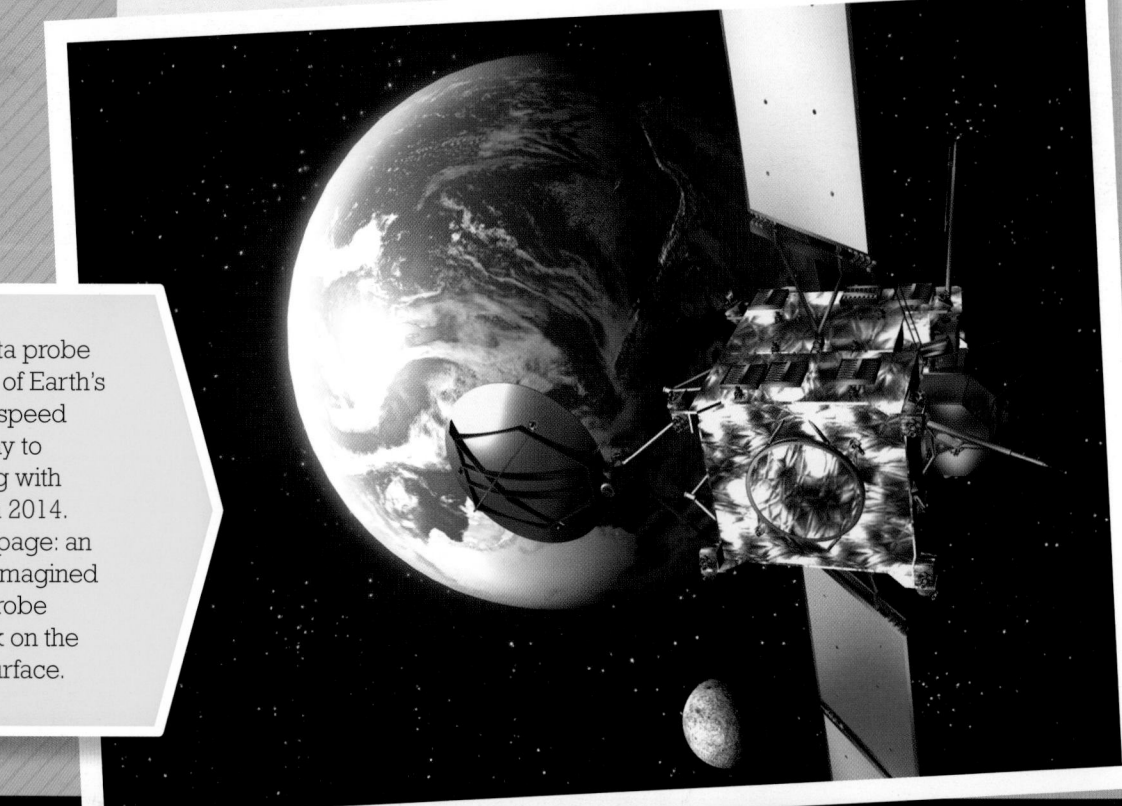

The Rosetta probe made use of Earth's gravity to speed it on its way to its meeting with a comet in 2014. Opposite page: an artist has imagined how the probe might look on the comet's surface.

Comet approach

The first approach to the comet takes place before Rosetta's cameras are activated. This means that everything depends on the observations of the comet's path made from Earth being absolutely accurate. As Rosetta closes in on the comet it will fire its braking rockets. Rosetta's thrusters will fire for several hours as it slows to match the comet's speed. Once the first images reach Earth the team will be able to make last minute adjustments to Rosetta's flight path. Eventually, if all goes well, it will enter an orbit just 25 kilometers (16 miles) above the comet's surface.

"It is absolutely mind blowing when you think of what we are going to do."

Rosetta project manager, John Elwood

Venetia, the Student Dust Counter

One of the instruments carried on board New Horizons (see page 27) is the Student Dust Counter (SDC), designed and built by students at the University of Colorado. It will measure the sizes of dust particles in space throughout the spacecraft's journey. The SDC was named Venetia after Venetia Burney, who suggested the name for Pluto when she was eleven.

Ice dwarves of the Kuiper belt

Some Kuiper belt objects are very big. One of the largest is Pluto, once considered to be the ninth planet in the solar system. In 2005 scientists announced that they had discovered a KBO that was bigger than Pluto.

Not even the powerful Hubble telescope can capture a clear image of distant Pluto. The smaller object seen below is Pluto's moon, Charon.

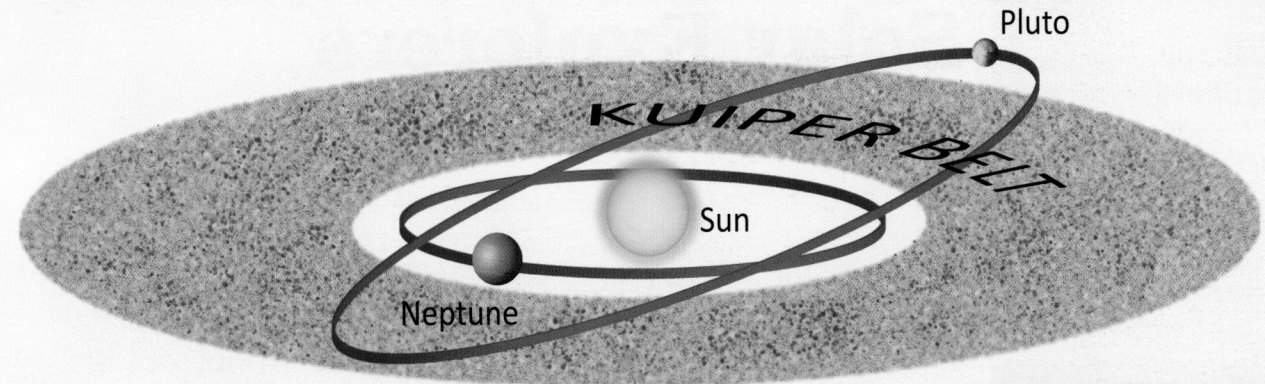

The icy objects in the Kuiper belt circle the solar system beyond the orbit of Neptune.

Dwarf planets

The discovery of Eris, as the new object was called, made scientists think again about what could actually be called a planet. They wondered if they should call Eris the tenth planet of the solar system. Instead of doing that they created a new class of dwarf planets. This would include Pluto, thereby changing its status as a planet. Today five dwarf planets are known: Ceres, Pluto, Haumea, Makemake, and Eris.

New Horizons

Launched at the beginning of 2006, the New Horizons space probe will encounter Pluto in 2015. This will be the first time this distant object will ever have been visited by a probe from Earth. For most of its long journey New Horizons is powered down into sleep mode to save energy, just as a computer monitor will go dark when it is not used for a while. Mission scientists will wake it up for 50 days each year to carry out instrument checks.

After its encounter with Pluto, New Horizons will continue on to investigate other KBOs. Investigator Alan Stern thinks it is important that we should send a spaceship to the Kuiper belt. He believes New Horizons will help us to gain a deeper understanding of the birth of the solar system.

"We're in the space exploration business and the outer solar system is a wild, woolly place. We haven't explored it very well."

Alan Stern

Solar Explorers

Without a doubt the most important object in space as far as people are concerned is the Sun — the star in the middle of the solar system. More than 99 percent of the material in the solar system is contained in the Sun and its powerful gravity holds everything else in place. There would be no life on Earth without its heat and light.

Genesis

Several missions have been launched to study the Sun. The Genesis probe was sent to capture material from the outer regions of the Sun's atmosphere and return it to Earth. These samples were collected using specially developed materials.

When the Genesis return capsule crashed back to Earth scientists were sure the mission would be a failure, but they still managed to find some usable samples.

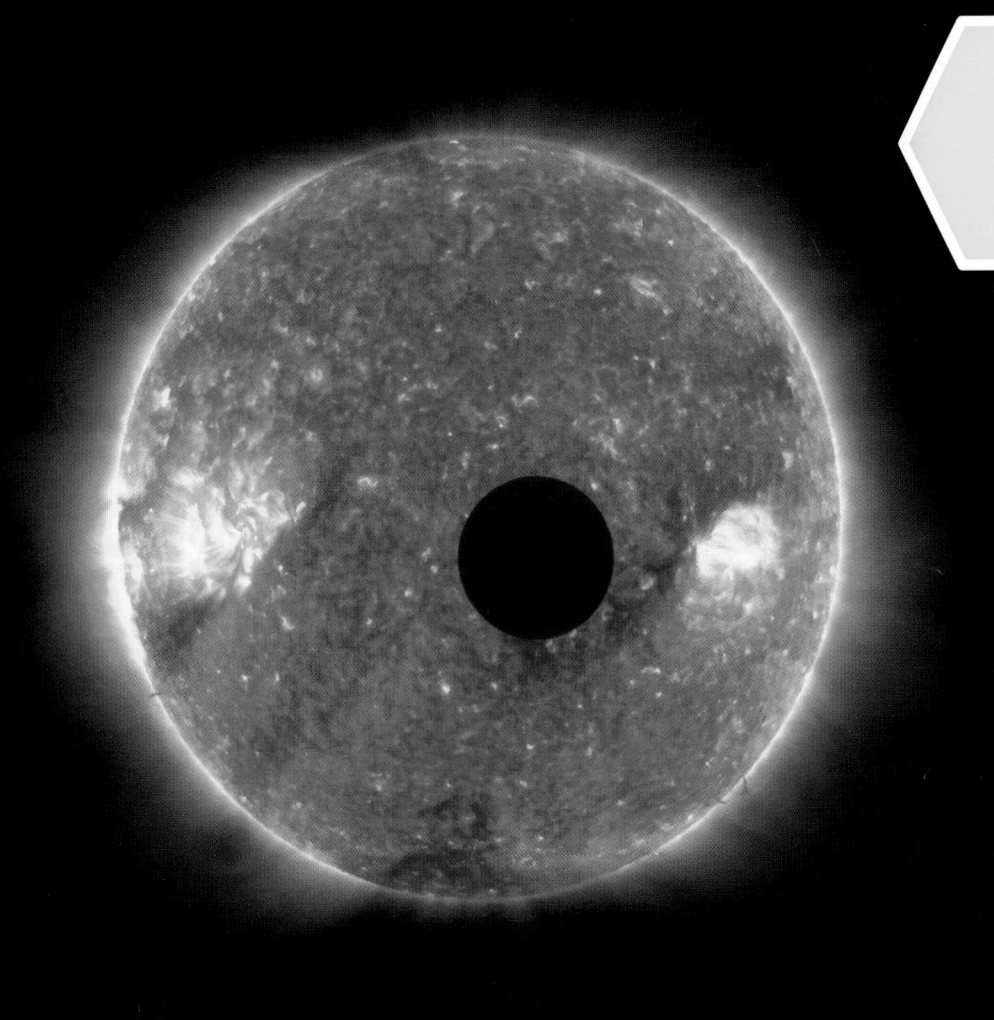

At the end of the collection period Genesis closed up and a sample return capsule was sent back to Earth. Unfortunately, when the capsule returned to Earth a design fault prevented its parachutes from opening. It crashed into the ground at high speed. Many of the collectors were shattered and scientists were concerned that the samples were contaminated. Luckily they determined that some samples were buried so deep in the collectors they could still be used for research.

Seeing in STEREO

The twin satellites of the STEREO (Solar Terrestrial Relations Observatory) mission are being used to capture never before seen images of the Sun. One satellite travels ahead of the Earth in its orbit while the other follows on behind. You might think of them as being like left and right eyes, working together to build up a stereoscopic (3D) image.

Coronal mass

Every so often the Sun throws off material in an explosion called a coronal mass ejection (CME). Each one contains the energy of millions of nuclear weapons and travels through space at 1,600,000 km/h (1,000,000 mph). Chris Davis of the Rutherford Appleton Laboratory in England is using STEREO to study CMEs. "If one of these clouds reaches the Earth, it has the potential to damage Earth-orbiting spacecraft, disrupt navigation systems, and cause power surges on the ground. We need to understand the extremes of this 'space weather' if mankind is to travel to the Moon and beyond."

SOHO

SOHO (the Solar and Heliospheric Observatory) is an international project operated jointly by the European Space Agency and NASA. Launched in 1995 it has been sending back huge amounts of data about the Sun to scientists on Earth. Using this information, researchers have been learning a great deal about our star and how it behaves.

SOHO being assembled before launch. The solar panels, seen flat against the sides at the bottom here, opened out once SOHO reached space.

CASE STUDY:

Saving SOHO

The SOHO mission almost came
to a disastrous end in 1998 when
a fault caused contact with the
satellite to be lost. Scientists tried
to make contact with SOHO using
NASA's Deep Space Network
(DSN) but there was no response.

What they thought was happening
was that SOHO had gone into a
spin with its solar panels nearly
edge on to the Sun. This meant
that it wasn't generating any
power. The deep chill of outer
space would freeze its batteries
and fuel. The scientists calculated
that there would be one point in
SOHO's orbit where the solar panels would get most light.

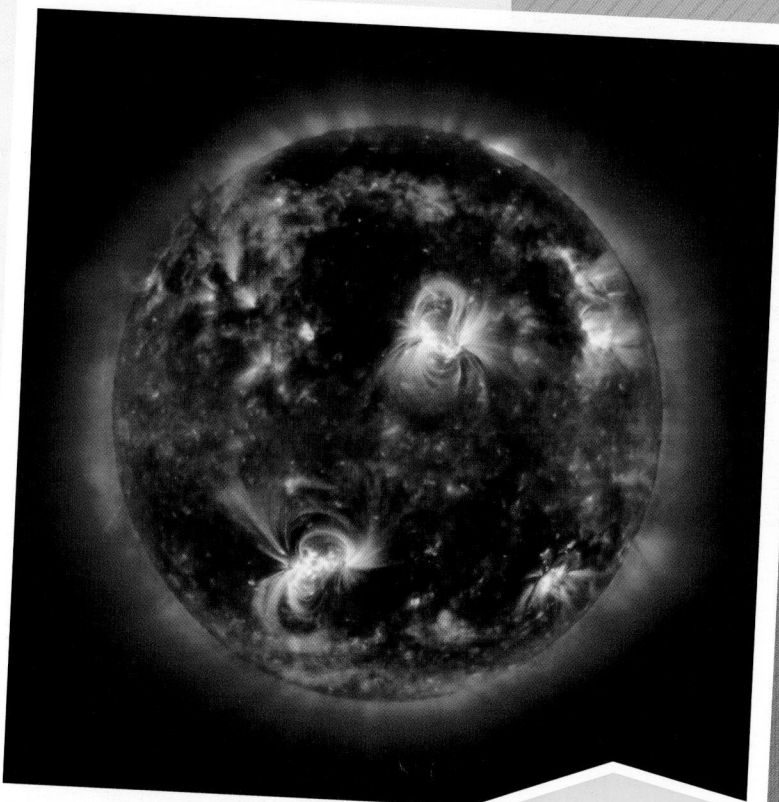

SOHO sent back never
before seen images of the
Sun. The colors here are
computer generated —
the Sun doesn't look blue
in space!

Breaking the silence

After six weeks of silence, the DSN picked up the first signals from
SOHO. This was the first sign that it could receive commands from the
ground. Immediately the team began to try and regain control of the
craft. John Credland, ESA head of science projects, said at the time,
"Recovery will be a slow and careful operation. The main thing is that
the spacecraft is now responding to us."

Return to life

Over the next three weeks the batteries slowly recharged. Eventually
there was enough power to begin to thaw out some of SOHO's
thrusters. Carefully using what little battery power they had, the team
made delicate adjustments using the available thrusters. Over nine
long days they stopped SOHO's spin and pointed it towards the Sun
once more.

By the end of 1998 all of the instruments on board SOHO were working
normally. Over ten years later SOHO is still helping scientists to
understand how our star works.

Other Stars, Other Worlds

For centuries people have wondered about the existence of other worlds. In 1992, astronomers using a radio telescope discovered two rocky planets orbiting a neutron star. Since then, more than 490 **exoplanets** (a planet around another star) have been discovered.

Giant planets

The first discovery of a planet orbiting a star similar to the Sun came in 1995. It was somewhere between half and twice as big as Jupiter. So far all the discoveries have been of giant worlds like this.

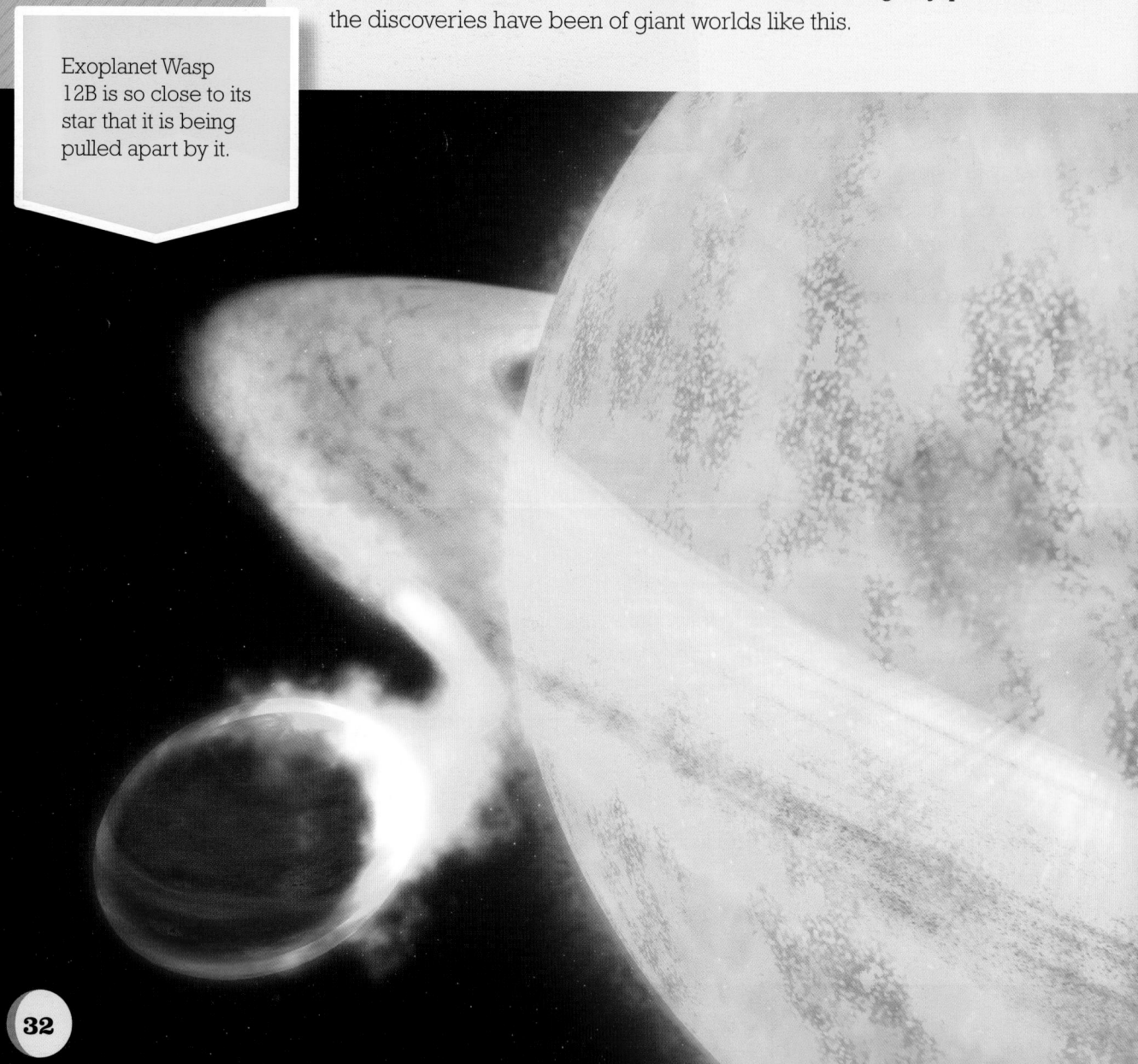

Exoplanet Wasp 12B is so close to its star that it is being pulled apart by it.

Professor Sara Seager is a world expert on exoplanets. She works with the Kepler Space Telescope.

Spitzer surprises

In 2005, the Spitzer Space Telescope captured infrared light from two exoplanets. This marked the first time that light from worlds beyond the solar system had been observed. Two years later Spitzer had detected evidence of water on an exoplanet and had been able to produce the first exoplanet temperature map.

Flying in formation

One of NASA's aims for the future is to launch five spacecraft that will work together as if they were a single huge telescope. The spaceships will likely fly in formation, about a kilometer (less than a mile) apart. Four will have telescopes and the fifth will combine the results from the other four. The power of this multi-telescope should be sufficient to pick up the faint light of an Earthlike planet against the brighter light of its parent star.

The hunt for other Earths

The search is on to find Earthlike worlds around other stars. A number of missions, using some of the most sensitive technology ever built, will join in the hunt. One of these is the Kepler Space Telescope, launched in 2009. Kepler is looking for planets using what is called the transit method. A transit occurs when a planet passes in front of its parent star. As it does so it blocks some of the light resulting in a slight dimming of the star. Kepler's sensitive instruments can detect this dimming if it takes place. Scientists can then use the measurements to calculate the size of the planet. Early indications in 2010 were that Kepler has indeed discovered many new worlds.

The flecks of light in this stunning Hubble image are not stars — they are unimaginably distant galaxies, each containing billions of stars.

Telescopic time machines

The fastest thing in the Universe is light. It speeds across space from the stars to us at an astonishing 300,000 kilometers per second (186,000 miles per second). Even more astonishing is that even at that huge speed it still takes light four years to make the trip from the *nearest* star, Proxima Centauri.

Across the Universe

Using a telescope shows us things that are not only very far away in space, but also distant in time. Light from the most distant galaxies set out on its journey across space billions of years before the Earth had even formed. Studying the light can help scientists understand how galaxies have changed over time.

Back to the beginning

Most scientists believe that the Universe came into existence in a Big Bang billions of years ago and it has been expanding ever since. Observations of deep space made by the Hubble Space Telescope and the WMAP Observatory have measured the faint radiation in space left over from the Big Bang. This has allowed scientists to estimate the age of the Universe. Currently the Universe is believed to be around 13.5 billion years old.

Furthest reaches

The Wide Field Camera 3 (WFC3) is the most advanced instrument aboard Hubble. It was installed during a space shuttle mission early in 2009. At the end of that year scientists obtained some remarkable images from the WFC3.

Shining faintly from the furthest reaches of the Universe are galaxies that are so far away light left them 13 billion years ago, just a few hundred million years after the Universe is thought to have begun. Marcella Carollo was a member of the survey team that put together the data from WFC3. She described the distant galaxies as "the very building blocks from which the great galaxies of today, like our own **Milky Way**, ultimately formed." The scientists combined the Hubble data with data from the Spitzer Space Telescope to estimate the age and size of the galaxies.

"To our surprise, the results show that these galaxies... must have started forming stars hundreds of millions of years earlier, pushing back the time of the earliest star formation in the Universe."

Ivo Labbe, Spitzer Space Telescope team member

A dark Universe

Scientists have calculated that 96 percent of the Universe is made up of dark matter and dark energy. So everything that we see and know, including stars, planets, animals, and people, accounts for less than a twentieth of the Universe.

These two galaxies are slowly colliding, pulled together by powerful gravitational forces. Over billions of years they will merge into one.

Where is everything?

One of the biggest mysteries for space scientists is trying to figure out where most of the Universe actually is. Their calculations of how much material there is in the Universe don't make any sense. Unless, that is, most of the Universe is invisible to us.

How to weigh a galaxy

Obviously it isn't possible to weigh a galaxy the same way you might weigh potatoes. However, galaxies spin and it is possible to measure how fast they are rotating. The speed of the spin depends on the amount of mass (material) in the galaxy. Knowing one it is possible to figure out the other.

The problem was that when scientists carried out their galaxy-weighing calculations the results didn't come out the right way. The calculations indicated that there was five or six times more matter than we could actually see. What can this mysterious dark matter possibly be? We only know about it because of its gravity. It emits no light or any other form of energy.

A Hubble image of a distant cluster of galaxies. Scientists believe invisible dark matter holds it all together.

Dark energy

As we saw earlier, the Universe is expanding. It isn't expanding steadily however. The rate of expansion is getting faster. The reasons for this are mysterious. Perhaps we don't understand gravity as well as we thought. Or perhaps there is a strange form of "dark energy" at work. Dark matter, it seems, pulls the Universe together, while dark energy pulls it apart.

Chandra

One of the satellites currently being used to try and solve the problem is NASA's Chandra X-ray Observatory. By observing distant clusters of galaxies Chandra has been able to see the effects of dark matter indirectly. Clouds of very hot gas lie between the galaxies in a cluster. The gases give off X-rays, which is how Chandra detects them. By observing how the gas clouds behave scientists can calculate where, and how massive, the dark matter is.

Being There

Most space scientists probably dream of actually being able to visit the stars and planets they study from afar. What does the future hold for human travel into deep space beyond the Moon?

The distant stars

The stars are so far away that we may never reach them. It is certainly unlikely that we would even attempt to at any time in the foreseeable future. Even Voyager 1, currently speeding from the solar system at over 60,000 kilometers per hour (37,282 miles per hour), would take around 75,000 years to cross the interstellar gulf to the nearest star.

Mission to Mars

Even a trip to the nearest planet, Mars, which some people think could take place around the 2030s, would mean a journey lasting more than a year for the crew. In May 2010 six volunteers were locked away in a mocked-up space module for over 500 days to simulate a flight to Mars.

How the volunteers react during the lengthy period they spend cooped up in the module will be of great help to mission planners for a real Mars mission. The mock spaceship also includes a Mars lander, and an area that has been made up to look like a Martian landscape. Three of the crew will also take part in a simulated Mars landing. Communication with the outside world will take place entirely by email to mimic the time delays there will be on an actual Mars voyage.

One day, perhaps, human explorers really will visit the surface of Mars.

Humans versus robots

Perhaps the biggest difficulty to be faced in the human exploration of space is the humans themselves. Humans are big and heavy, they need food, water, and air to breathe, they need to be protected against radiation in space. And eventually they want to come home again! All of this means having to build big powerful rockets to boost everything into space. At the moment, it is much more efficient to carry out our exploration of the Universe using telescopes and robot space probes that don't eat, sleep, or get bored on long journeys, and which can travel to places no human could survive.

Is there anyone out there?

Is it possible that one day our probes will send back evidence that there are other living things in the Universe? Astrobiology is the study of the origin, evolution, and future of life in the Universe.

Three questions

NASA's Astrobiology Program looks for answers to three fundamental questions:

- How does life begin and evolve?
- Is there life beyond Earth?
- If there is, how can we detect it?

Experts in astronomy and astrophysics, Earth and planetary sciences, microbiology, evolutionary biology and **cosmochemistry** are all involved in this fascinating and cutting-edge branch of space exploration. Several space missions play a part in astrobiology research, such as the Spitzer and Kepler telescopes hunting for Earthlike planets, and the Mars rovers searching for traces of life on Mars.

Europa

Europa is one of Jupiter's larger moons (it is one of the four first seen by Galileo). Its surface is made of ice and scientists believe that there may be an ocean of liquid water underneath. Some astrobiologists think that there may be life in that ocean. Finding out will be tricky as it will involve not only a journey to Europa, but also having to drill as much as 100 kilometers (62 miles) through the ice. So far the deepest well drilled on Earth has been just 10.6 kilometers (6.5 miles) deep.

What secrets lie beneath the icy surface of Europa?

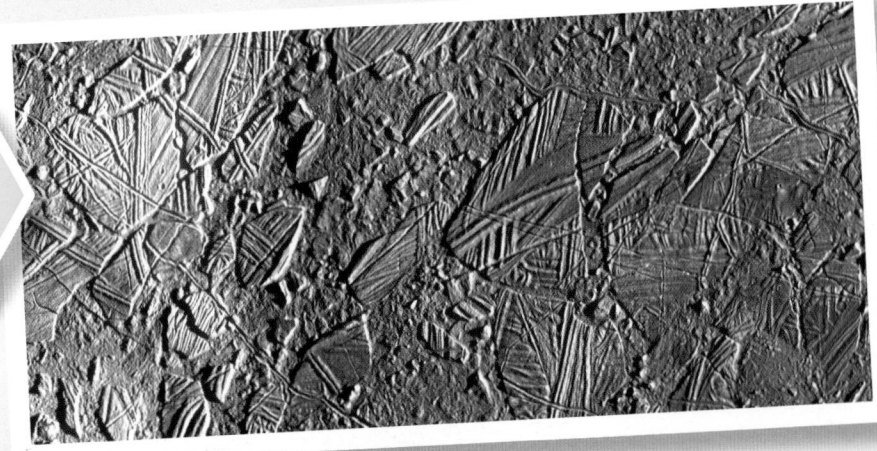

There is no reason to believe that Earth is the only place in the Universe where life has appeared. Just because we haven't detected it yet doesn't mean that it isn't there. It isn't possible to travel to the stars looking for life but we might still be able to find signs of it.

SETI

SETI is the Search for Extraterrestrial Intelligence. Scientists are looking for life in other parts of the Universe by trying to find evidence of its technology. Radio telescopes are being used in an attempt to pinpoint evidence of transmissions from alien beings. So far, the search has proved fruitless. We have sent messages but no one has answered… at least not yet.

These are radio telescopes in the Allen Telescope Array in California. They are part of SETI's mission to detect signals from alien civilizations.

WORD STATION
cosmochemistry branch of chemistry that deals with the chemistry of space

Timeline of Space Exploration

2296 BCE	Chinese astronomers make the first recorded observation of a comet.
763 BCE	Astronomers in Babylon (present-day Iraq) record seeing an eclipse of the Sun.
270 BCE	Aristarchus says the Sun is bigger than the Earth and the Earth goes around it.
1609	Galileo Galilei builds one of the first telescopes and begins his groundbreaking discoveries.
1655	Christiaan Huygens improves the design of the telescope and discovers the rings of Saturn.
1687	Isaac Newton explains his ideas about gravity.
1781	William Herschel discovers there are star systems beyond our galaxy.
1903	Russian scientist Konstantin Tsiolkovsky claims that space travel will be possible one day; later that year the Wright Brothers make the first powered flight.
1915	Proxima Centauri, the nearest star to the Earth other than the Sun, is discovered.
1932	Karl Jansky tells the world about cosmic radio waves.
1957	The USSR launches the first satellite, Sputnik 1.
1957	Laika the dog becomes the first living creature to orbit the Earth aboard Sputnik 2.
1959	The space probe Luna 3 sends back the first images of the far side of the Moon.
1961	Aboard his Vostok space capsule, Major Yuri Gagarin of the USSR becomes the first man to orbit the Earth.
February 1966	Luna 9 makes the first controlled landing on the surface of the Moon.
1968	The crew of Apollo 8 are the first people from Earth to orbit the Moon.
1969	Apollo 11 astronauts Neil Armstrong and Edwin (Buzz) Aldrin are the first men to walk on the Moon.

1970	Venera 7 is the first probe to successfully land on the surface of Venus.
April 1971	Salyut 1, the first space station to orbit the Earth, is launched.
November 1971	Mariner 9 reaches Mars and becomes the first space probe from Earth to orbit another planet.
1972	Apollo 17 returns to Earth from the Moon — there have been no more Moon missions to date.
1976	Viking 1 makes the first successful landing on Mars.
1980	Voyager 1 reaches Saturn and sends back the first detailed pictures of the ringed planet.
1989	Voyager 2 sends back the first close-up images of the planet Neptune.
April 25, 1990	The Hubble Space Telescope is carried into orbit aboard the space shuttle Discovery.
1992	NASA launches SETI, the Search for Extraterrestrial Intelligence.
1997	The remote-controlled Sojourner rover on Mars becomes the first human-made craft to travel over the surface of another planet.
2000	The first crew begins working aboard the International Space Station.
2005	The Huygens space probe lands on the surface of Titan, one of the moons of Saturn — it is the most distant landing ever made by an object from Earth.
January 2006	Samples from the Stardust mission to Comet Wild 2 reach Earth.
October 2006	The twin STEREO space probes are launched to study the Sun.
*2011	MESSENGER is due to enter orbit around Mercury.
2011	Russia plans to launch Phobos-Grunt, a sample return mission to one of the moons of Mars.
2014	Rosetta is due to makes its rendezvous with a comet.
2015	New Horizon will make a flyby of Pluto and the Kuiper belt.
2020	India and Japan plan manned landings on the Moon.

* Dates in 2011 and beyond are planned, but are subject to change.

Glossary

asteroid sometimes called minor planets, these are rocky objects orbiting the Sun in the solar system. Asteroids vary greatly in size.

astronomer person who studies objects and matter that are outside Earth's atmosphere

astronomy branch of science that studies everything beyond the Earth's atmosphere, including planets, stars, and galaxies

atmosphere layer of gases or other objects in space that surround a planet

black hole region of space left by a star collapsing at the end of its life; a black hole's gravity is so powerful that not even light can escape it

comet fairly small, just a few kilometers across, icy object that orbits the Sun; when a comet approaches the Sun it produces a long tail of gas and dust

constellation pattern of stars in the night sky

cosmochemistry branch of chemistry that deals with the chemistry of space

electromagnetic spectrum range of radiation that travels through space in the form of waves; radio waves are the longest and X-rays and gamma rays are the shortest

exoplanet planet outside the solar system orbiting a star other than the Sun

galaxy collection of billions of stars

gravity force of attraction between all objects in the Universe; the more massive an object is the greater the force of gravity it exerts

gravity assist using the gravity of a planet to change the speed and flight path of a space probe

greenhouse gas gas in the atmosphere that absorbs heat and reflects it back to the surface rather than letting it escape into space

interstellar space space between the stars

Kuiper belt part of the solar system beyond the orbit of the planet Neptune; it is thought to be occupied by millions of comets and minor planets

meteorite space rock that crashes onto the surface of another larger object in space such as a moon or planet

Milky Way galaxy that contains the Sun and solar system

orbit move around an object in a circular manner, or the path on which an object moves around another object

sol word for a single day on Mars. A sol is 35 minutes, 39 seconds longer than a day on Earth.

solar panel device that converts light energy into electrical energy

solar system our Sun and its family of planets, asteroids, and other objects that orbit around it

space probe unmanned spaceship sent out to explore space

Universe everything that exists; all of space and everything in it

Find Out More

Books

Dowswell, Paul. *First Encyclopedia of Space.* Tulsa, OK: EDC, 2010.

Harrison, Paul. *Space.* New York, NY: Rosen, 2008.

Parker, Steve. *Space Exploration.* Broomall, PA: Mason Crest, 2011.

Schneider, Howard. *Backyard Guide to the Night Sky.* Washington, DC: National Geographic, 2009.

Websites

www.nasa.gov
The homepage of NASA, an excellent starting-off point for information on all aspects of space exploration.

www.esa.int/esaCP/index.html
The website of the European Space Agency – ESA.

www.newton.dep.anl.gov/askasci/astron98.htm
Hundreds of questions and answers from the Ask A Scientist Astronomy Archive at the USA's Argonne National Laboratory.

http://hubblesite.org
The latest news and findings from the Hubble Space Telescope and links to a wealth of information on astronomy.

www.iwaswondering.org/heidi_homepage.html
Space scientist Heidi Hammel's kid friendly guide to space exploration.

www.skyandtelescope.com
The website of *Sky and Telescope*, the magazine for the amateur astronomer.

Places to visit

Smithsonian's National Air and Space Museum, Washington, D.C.
www.nasm.si.edu

Visit the nation's most comprehensive museum of space, the
Kennedy Space Center located in Orlando, Florida. While
there you can tour NASA's launch and landing facilities.
www.kennedyspacecenter.com/visit-us.aspx

Index